calm
colouring

soothe your soul

Jacqui Lenaghan

LOVE&WRITE
PUBLISHING

First published by Love and Write Publishing
PO Box 252
Summer Hill NSW 2130
Australia
www.loveandwrite.com.au

A copy of this publication can be found in the National Library
of Australia.

ISBN 978-0-9923070-4-2

Cover design by Jessica Le
Text layout by Sonya Murphy
Printed in China

Introduction

Whether playing with a multitude of colourful fabrics for my next quilt, cutting or buying some fresh flowers to brighten up the house or just getting out my coloured pencils and colouring in a design; I find colour can be a great healer and provide a fabulous opportunity for play.

I love designing and sewing new quilt patterns with a multitude of colourful fabrics and designing and then colouring the patterns can be a great first step in learning this wonderful craft.

By creating this colouring book I want to combine the relaxation of colour and the inspiration of quilt design to invoke a unique calming experience that everyone, from experienced quilt makers to novice colour enthusiasts, can enjoy.

I hope you enjoy colouring in these lovely quilt designs and that they may inspire you to create your own handmade quilts.

Happy colouring!
Jacqui Lenaghan

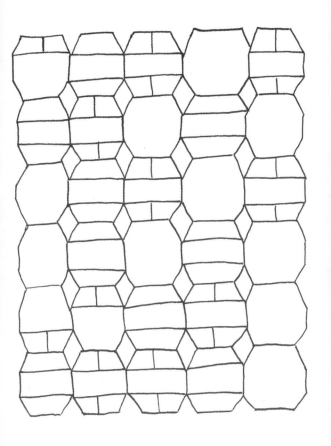

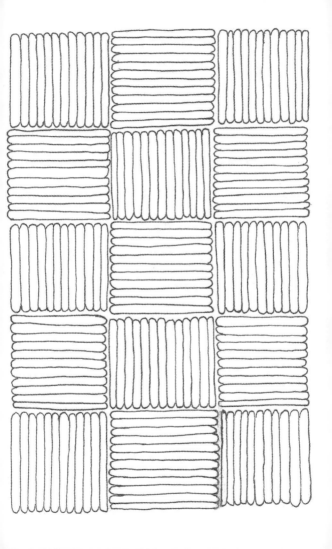

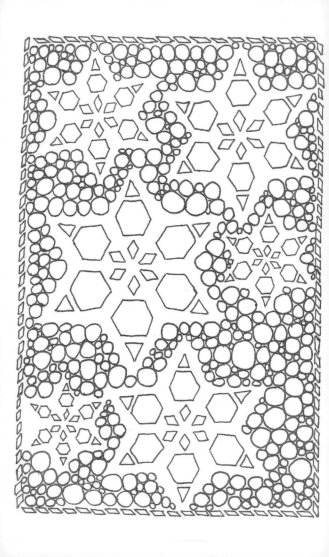

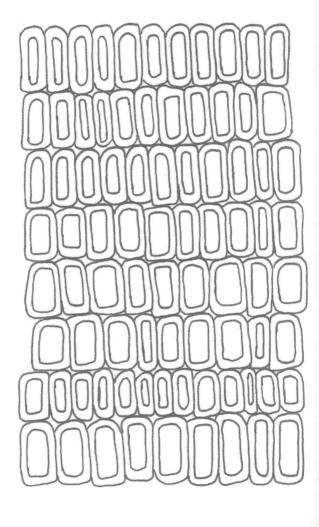

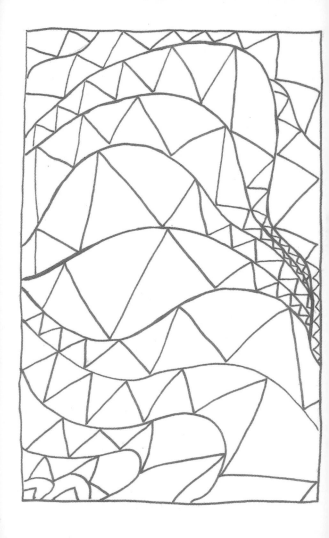

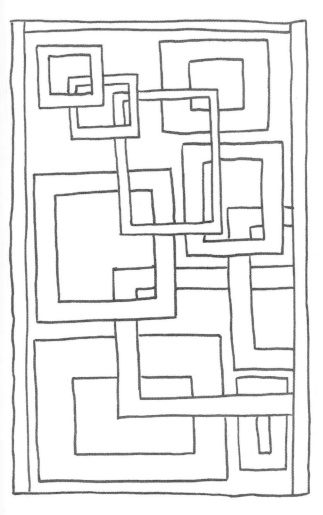

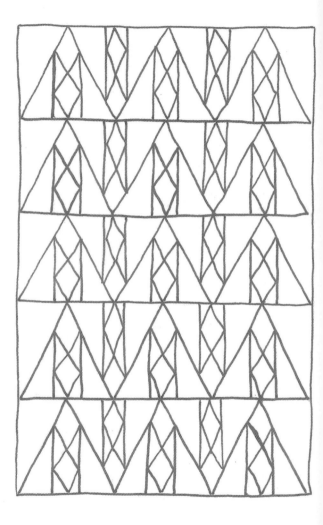

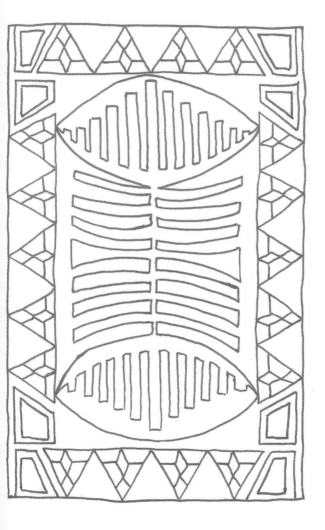

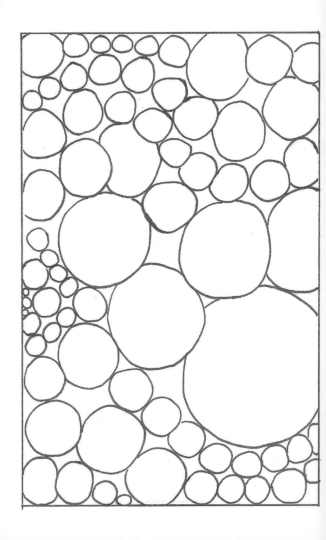

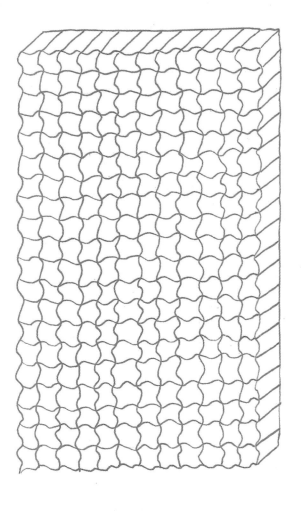

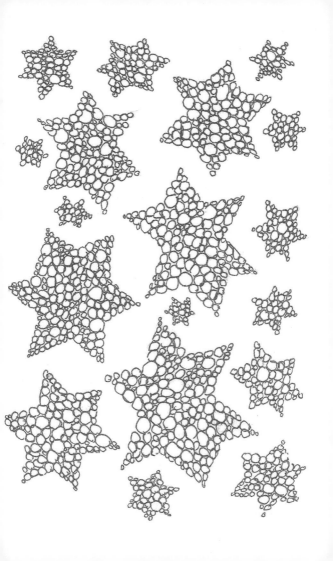

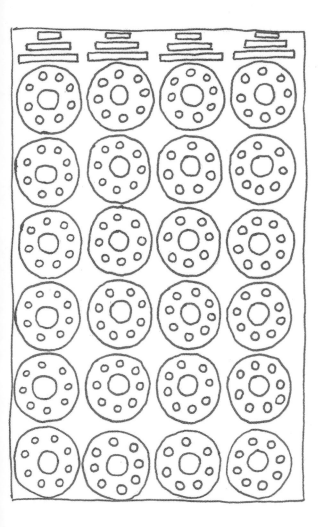

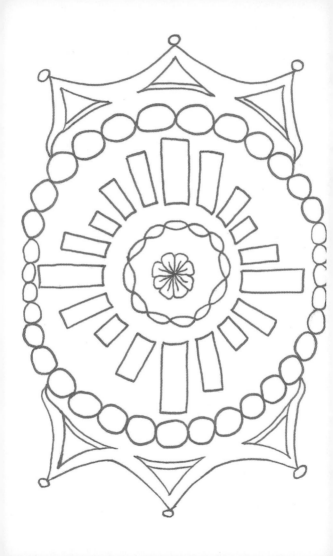

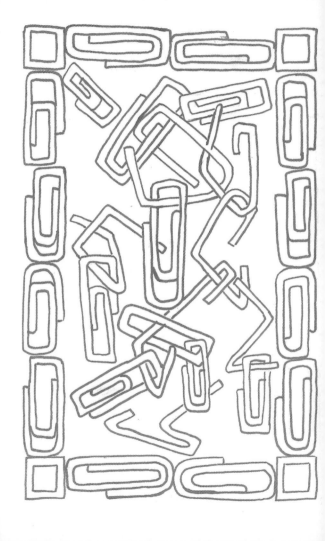

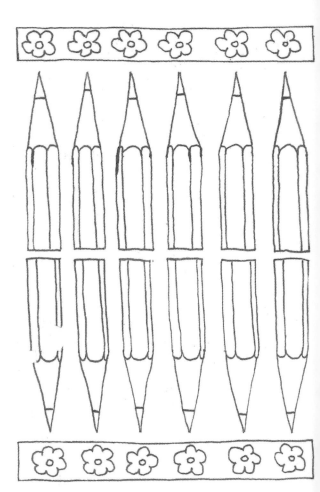

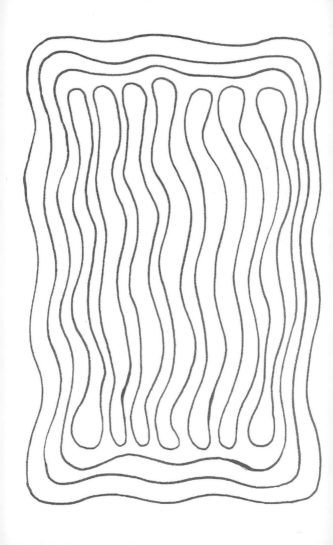

About the Author

Calm Colouring is the perfect creative outlet for quilt makers and colour connoisseurs alike and quilt designer Jacqui Lenaghan has created 100 amazing tessellated designs for the first time in sketch form for you to add your own colour palette.

Jacqui has brought her amazing life experiences and love of art to her designs via the unique and vibrant fabrics (as well as antiques) she has collected on her travels to Eastern Europe and the Middle East. She has always been fascinated by the exquisite and original hand-sewn designs produced by women in Middle Eastern refugee camps – amazed at how they are able to produce beautiful works of art in the face of adversity.

She made her first quilt by hand – no sewing machines. Each of her patchwork patterns are drawn by hand and she is developing her own line of original quilt designs.

Jacqui has a Bachelor of Arts degree majoring in English & History. She currently resides in the NSW Southern Highlands. She finds colouring a joyful experience and the first step in learning a new craft or perfecting a long-term hobby. This book provides you with fresh mandala like patterns to colour for mindful stress relief and may even provide the inspiration for your next quilt project!

For more information about Jacqui and her quilting go to: www.patchworkbox.com.au